The Manhattan Project:
A Secret Wartime Mission

Edited by Kenneth M. Deitch

Discovery Enterprises, Ltd.
Lowell, Massachusetts

© Discovery Enterprises, Ltd., Lowell, MA 1995

ISBN 1-878668-41-2 paperback edition
Library of Congress Catalog Card Number 94-71896

10   9   8   7   6   5   4   3   2

Printed in the United States of America

Subject Reference Guide:

The Manhattan Project: A Secret Wartime Mission,
edited by Kenneth M. Deitch
Manhattan Project – History
Nuclear Fission – Science
Atomic Bomb – World War II History

Photo Credits

Cover Photographs

Foreground, left to right: General Leslie R. Groves and
J. Robert Oppenheimer. Courtesy of Harry S. Truman Library,
Independence, Missouri.

Background, left: Trinity, thirty seconds after detonation.
Courtesy of Los Alamos National Laboratory, Los Alamos, New Mexico.

Other Photographs

Page 4. Courtesy of Los Alamos Historical Museum Photo Archives,
Los Alamos, New Mexico

Pages 31 and 36. Courtesy of Los Alamos National Laboratory

Editorial Note

In the readings, a full line of dots indicates the deletion of at least
an entire paragraph. Except as noted on pages 25 and 43, an
ellipsis (. . .) indicates a deletion by the editor within a paragraph.

Table of Contents

Checkpoint at the main gate of the secret wartime weapons laboratory located high on a New Mexican mesa, at a place called Los Alamos

Introduction

by

Kenneth M. Deitch

During World War II, a top-secret mission was undertaken to develop the atomic bomb. It subsequently came to be known as the Manhattan Project. This small book, an anthology, introduces it. Most of the selections that follow are firsthand accounts.

The mission culminated in the summer of 1945 when America successfully tested one atomic device and, soon thereafter, dropped two atomic bombs as acts of war. The test took place on July 16 in a remote section of New Mexico. The two bombs were dropped over Japan, the first on Hiroshima on August 6 and the second on Nagaski on August 9. Both cities were devastated. Within a few days, Japan surrendered. Because victory over Nazi Germany had been achieved three months earlier, World War II was finally over.

The Manhattan Project was mostly an American undertaking. Still, it had important international components. Both Great Britain and Canada were participants, and a number of the project's scientists were refugees from Nazi-dominated Europe. Moreover, the intellectual foundation that made the atomic bomb possible was largely a series of accomplishments, begun in the 1890s, by European and British scientists.

Two major scientific watersheds were reached in the 1930s. One came in 1932 when James Chadwick, an Englishman, discovered a new subatomic particle, the neutron. Another arrived late in 1938 when Otto Hahn and Fritz Strassmann, both German chemists, split the uranium atom. But they did so without quite being able to provide a cogent explanation of the bewildering event. Two other European scientists, Lise Meitner and Otto R. Frisch—aunt and nephew—did provide it.

The process of splitting the atom was named fission. When it takes place, energy is released in accordance with Albert Einstein's now legendary formula $E = mc^2$ or, in words, energy equals mass times the velocity of light squared, the variables expressed in mutually compatible units. What is so astounding about this formula is the disparity implied between the enormous amount of energy emerging and the small quantity of matter serving as its source. Atomic bombs graphically illustrate the point. In each of the original bombs, the explosive core —the part packing the deadly wallop—was around the size of a grapefruit.

Toward the end of the 1930s, knowledge about fission and hostility in international relations were accelerating side by side. In this environment, scientists began to inform their governments about the new discoveries and where they might lead. In America, an early communication between the scientific community and the federal government—not the first but certainly the most celebrated—was the famous letter from Einstein to President Franklin D. Roosevelt. Leo Szilard, a scientist originally from Hungary but by then living in the United States, was the moving force behind the letter, both encouraging Einstein to prepare it and helping him to do so. The letter alerted the President to the threat posed by atomic energy in the wrong hands and stirred him to initiate the government's exploration of the possibility of developing the atomic bomb. Begun on a small scale, the effort soon had a cryptic designation: S-1.

Not until almost two years to the day after receiving Einstein's letter did the President decide that the government should make a major commitment. His decision of October 9, 1941, was based upon a recommendation from Vannevar Bush, director of the Office of Scientific Research and Development (OSRD), who was the President's senior advisor on these matters. Bush had been strongly influenced by a secret British document known as the MAUD report. It was the result of some excellent scientific work, and it concluded that a bomb was possible. But Britain did not have the luxury of undertaking such an uncertain venture, and so the responsibility fell mostly upon America.

An ongoing impetus to those administering the project was the fear that Germany might be developing an atomic bomb of its own. In fact, there was no such danger. But only quite late in the war did the Allies learn this information definitively. What limited efforts the Germans had begun, they had abandoned by the fall of 1942.

In the work proceeding in America, a crucial step was taken in June of 1942. A special section was established within the Army Corps of Engineers that was soon to assume all day-to-day responsibility for developing the atomic bomb. It was named the Manhattan Engineer District and called, for short, the MED. In time, the undertaking to build the bomb came to be referred to predominantly as the Manhattan Project. In some quarters, the project continued to be called S-1 throughout the war and even beyond its end.

Much of the bomb's fundamental science developed along four overlapping pathways of investigation; the early exploration along each predated the MED. One concerned the separation of uranium's isotopes. As found in nature, uranium is a blend of three slightly different types of atoms; each variant is referred to as an isotope. Early on it was discovered that the explosive core of a bomb based on uranium must be composed of the isotope referred to as U-235 which constitutes only about seven-tenths of one percent of natural uranium.

Separating and collecting the U-235 became a monumentally challenging task. It was carried on in gargantuan facilities located in eastern Tennessee, near Knoxville, at a site originally named the Clinton Engineer Works after a small town nearby. Eventually the area came to be called Oak Ridge.

The second basic scientific pathway led to the initial self-sustaining chain reaction, a process of neutron-induced atom-splitting that races through a myriad of generations, mush-rooming as it goes. The first self-sustaining chain reaction was achieved on December 2, 1942, by a team of scientists led by Enrico Fermi. They were working at the University of Chicago in an organization named, somewhat deceptively, the Metallurgical Laboratory and routinely called the Met Lab. Fermi referred to the large structure housing the chain reaction as a "pile." This pile was more the forerunner of the modern nuclear reactor than of the atomic bomb itself, but it was an important step on the way to both.

Along the third pathway, plutonium was developed. Although people commonly refer to "the" atomic bomb, right from the start there were two types, one fueled by U-235, the other, by plutonium.

Except for some trace quantities, plutonium is not one of the ninety-two elements existing in nature. For practical pur-poses, it is man-made. It was initially created at the University of California at Berkeley late in February of 1941 by chemist Glenn T. Seaborg and his colleagues. It was quickly discovered to be, like U-235, highly fissionable. In addition, it happened to be a by-product of a chain-reacting pile. Therefore, it offered a second possible path to an atomic bomb, a chance to obtain one even if all efforts to isolate U-235 failed. To fabricate plutonium would also take gargantuan facilities. They were constructed in the state of Washington, along a stretch of the

Columbia River, near the towns of Hanford and Richland. The site was soon officially designated the Hanford Engineer Works.

The fourth pathway of investigation concerned the concept of critical mass in relation to an atomic bomb. In England, in 1940, Otto Frisch and Rudolf E. Peierls put into writing the insight that some minimum amount of U-235 had to be present in order to achieve detonation. This quantity came to be called the critical mass. Frisch and Peierls's idea was that "[t]he bomb would. . . be manufactured in two (or more) parts, each being less than the critical size. . . .The bomb would be provided with a mechanism that brings the two parts together when the bomb is intended to go off." In a slightly different way, the concept applies to plutonium as well. Determining the critical mass of U-235 and of plutonium became major preoccupations for a number of the Manhattan Project's scientists.

A multitude of individuals worked on the Manhattan Project. At one extreme in the hierarchy of authority were many thousands who labored diligently while remaining unaware of the project's goal and its immense scope. At the other extreme was a committee that came to be called the Top Policy Group. Although it never convened in its entirety, it was, in essence, the Manhattan Project's governing board. The members were President Roosevelt; Vice President Henry A. Wallace; Secretary of War Henry L. Stimson; Army Chief of Staff George C. Marshall; Vannevar Bush; and James B. Conant. A chemist and president of Harvard University, Conant was Bush's close colleague in mobilizing science to serve Allied interests.

Among those bearing day-to-day responsibility, two people have properly been singled out over the years as the project's leaders. One was a career Army officer named Leslie R. Groves. A 1918 graduate of the United States Military Academy at West Point, he was hoping to be assigned overseas when, in

September of 1942, he was placed in charge of the MED. As encouragement, one of his superior officers told him: "If you do this job right, it will win the war."

The other central figure was J. Robert Oppenheimer, a brilliant American-born physicist. He had graduated from Harvard in three years, had obtained his graduate training in England and Europe, and had been a member of the faculty at both the University of California at Berkeley and the California Institute of Technology since the late 1920s. "Oppie" was his nickname. He had worked on some of the pre-MED, government-sponsored, bomb-related research. As the Manhattan Project was getting into high gear, he was selected, at the age of thirty-eight, for its preeminent scientific assignment: director of the weapons laboratory to be established at a remote location in New Mexico known as Los Alamos.

All of the prior-stage efforts were to come together at Los Alamos. The laboratory's specific purpose was to puzzle out the meticulous details of designing and constructing the first bombs. It accomplished this mission in the twenty-eight months between Oppenheimer's arrival on March 15, 1943, and the successful test of the first atomic device on July 16, 1945.

The laboratory was located high on a secluded mesa, about thirty-five miles northwest of Santa Fe. Since 1917, Los Alamos Ranch School, a private residential boys' school, had occupied a small portion of the mesa. After the site was selected, the school had to evacuate its campus on short notice.

The site became a covert Army base. Sealed off from the outside world by barbed wire, the base contained an inner sanctum, known as the Tech Area, itself sealed off from the rest of the base, also by barbed wire. The facility's original official designation was Site Y; informally, those present came to refer to it as the Hill. At first Los Alamos was a small community, but it grew rapidly. Some came alone; others, with their families. Some arrived for short stays; others, for the duration. The population in the summer of 1945 is estimated to have reached around 5,000.

For all, it was an unusual community. Rare was the resident over forty. A few of the higher-ranking rated the posher accommodations along what came to be called "Bathtub Row" because the houses had the luxury of bathtubs. But most lived in newly-constructed and strictly utilitarian housing. Roads were not paved and became muddy when the weather was wet, dusty when it was dry.

Concern for security was pervasive and was reflected in a variety of precautions and prohibitions. Outgoing mail had to be dropped off unsealed so that the censors could review it. Incoming mail had to be sent to the communal address, Box 1663 in Santa Fe. Travel for pleasure beyond the outer fence was not forbidden, but it was restricted. Other than high-ranking officials, visitors were not permitted.

In short, life on the base was spartan, but the scientists were making their wartime contribution to the Allied cause while spouses—many of whom had jobs at the laboratory—and children in residence were generally resourceful in adapting to the adventure.

The central scientific challenge at Los Alamos was to develop the expertise to detonate an atomic bomb at a chosen time and place. The technique first focused upon was called the gun method. It produces a critical mass when a projectile carrying one subcritical bundle of fissionable material is fired into a muzzle-like receptacle containing one or more other such bundles. The gun method was initially expected to work with both fissionable materials, but in the summer of 1944, scientists learned that it would only be viable with U-235, not with plutonium.

If the plutonium in preparation around Hanford were to be usable in a bomb, another method of detonation would have to be developed. A second, more complicated method had been under study. It was called implosion. Its basic strategy is to make a below-critical sphere of plutonium critical, not by bringing it together with another bundle of plutonium, but rather, by compressing it powerfully, rapidly, and uniformly. However, in the summer of 1944, the scientists were far from having mastered implosion's intricacies. They worked feverishly over the next year to do so. By mid-July of 1945, they were ready to test a device based on implosion and plutonium. They could not be certain of the outcome in advance but were confident that, if it worked, not only would a bomb based on implosion and plutonium be ready for deployment in war, but so would one based on the gun method and U-235, even without testing.

The incentive to conduct a test by mid-July was enormous. An international conference was scheduled to begin just around then in a suburb of Berlin named Potsdam. Its principals were the leaders of the United States, Great Britain, and the Soviet Union. If an atomic bomb were part of the arsenal, it would immeasurably strengthen the Anglo-American hand in dealing with the Soviet Union. Before the Potsdam Conference's adjournment, American and British representatives would know.

More than a year before the test, its planning had begun. The location eventually selected was a large, barren tract of New Mexican desert in the northwest corner of the Alamorgordo Bombing Range, something over two hundred miles south of Los Alamos. Oppenheimer named both the test and the test site Trinity. At a spot designated Ground Zero, a steel tower, one hundred feet tall, was assembled. Atop it was a platform supporting a small shack that would shield the device.

As the test's long-awaited moment approached, many who had been involved in one aspect or another of the project gathered. Groves, Oppenheimer, and Groves's deputy, Brigadier General Thomas F. Farrell, were present. So were Bush, Conant, and quite a number of the other distinguished scientists whose brilliance had brought the project this far.

Shortly before sunrise on Monday, July 16, 1945, the physicist broadcasting the countdown punctuated its termination: "Now!" The resulting light, heat, sound, and blast imparted to those witnessing the event an overwhelming introduction to the realities of atomic energy, an experience not ever to be forgotten. Individuals' exact reactions varied. For Oppenheimer, the encounter brought to mind a line from Hindu scripture, "Now I am become death, the destroyer of worlds." Farrell was moved to exclaim to Groves, "The war is over," to which Groves responded, "Yes, after we drop two bombs on Japan."

Opinions differed about how to proceed once a working atomic bomb was in hand. Some wanted to try to avoid its use by somehow demonstrating vividly to the Japanese its awesome destructive capacity in an effort to convince them to surrender. Although that view received a hearing at very high levels, it did not prevail. As a formality, when the Potsdam Declaration was issued towards the end of July, it did warn that unless Japan's government were "to proclaim now the unconditional surrender of all Japanese armed forces," Japan would face "prompt and utter destruction." But in the context of events, no one uninformed about Trinity was likely to have truly comprehended the message, despite the clarity of the language.

Meanwhile, the enormous momentum that had been generated pressed forward. When bombs were ready, they were used. There was no real chance it would be otherwise.

The bomb dropped on Hiroshima incorporated the gun method of detonation and U-235. It was called Little Boy. The one dropped on Nagasaki, referred to as Fat Man, was based on implosion and plutonium. Many years afterward, the number of deaths from the bombing of Hiroshima was estimated to have reached 140,000 as of the end of 1945 and 200,000 as of five years later. For Nagasaki, the comparable numbers were 70,000 and 140,000. And the dying did not stop after five years. In addition, legions of individuals, who were injured by an atomic bomb but not killed, had their lives impaired in varying degrees of severity, sometimes gruesomely.

The immediate result of dropping those two bombs was that World War II, so agonizing to so many for so long, finally ended. How long it would otherwise have taken to conclude the fighting, what the total human suffering would have been, and how that suffering would have been shared between the combatants were then—and remain—imponderables. But once the Manhattan Project produced those bombs, victory came to America and its Allies—and defeat to Japan—swiftly and decisively.

For the longer term, two other things happened. The number of people who could be killed at a single stroke vastly increased, and the awful ravages of radiation became an ominous menace for survivors. By raising the grim horrors attainable in war to new levels, these changes constituted the crossing of a threshold. The crossing of that threshold in the summer of 1945 has had a profound impact, in ways both perilous and promising, on how, since then, history has been unfolding.

Spreading the Word

A major scientific breakthrough on the path to the atomic bomb was the discovery, made in Europe late in 1938, that uranium is fissionable. The story spread rapidly throughout the international scientific community and, before long, captured the attention of journalists. Here is an article that soon appeared in Time.

Source: *Time*, March 13, 1939, p. 46. Copyright © 1939 TIME INC. Reprinted by permission.

Six weeks ago a report reached the U. S. about an atomic explosion which took place in a Berlin laboratory—the most violent atomic explosion ever accomplished by human agency (TIME, Feb. 6). This news, known then only to a few insiders, streaked over the physical world like a meteor. By last week a half-dozen leading science journals were popping with reports confirming, extending or interpreting the original phenomenon.

Dr. Otto Hahn, 60, of Germany's Kaiser Wilhelm Institute, and his co-worker, F. Strassmann, had bombarded uranium with neutrons. In the products of bombardment they found something which seemed to be atoms of barium. This barium was the clue to something terrific. For the huge uranium atom, heaviest of the 92 standard elements, weighs 238 units.* The barium atom weighs 137 units. Since the barium could have originated only as a fragment of the big uranium atom, it was logical to suppose that the latter had cracked asunder, in two nearly equal parts. The release of atomic energy was 200,000,000 electron-volts. Heavy atoms had been "chipped"

---

* The unit is approximately the weight of the hydrogen atom (or, precisely, 1/16 the weight of the oxygen atom).

before—that is, forced to throw off small particles like neutrons —but this was the first time they had been cracked in two.

This discovery has already brought into play new words, familiar in other fields of science but not so in atomic physics. The splitting of the uranium nucleus is described as a "fission," which, in biology, means division of an organism into two or more parts. The big nucleus has been compared to a "droplet." When a neutron of the right energy strikes it, the new energy is shared by all the components of the nucleus so that the "surface tension" fails to hold it together. Therefore it splits.

. . . Last week the "fission" of the uranium atom definitely looked like a find of Nobel Prize calibre. But present German law forbids Germans to accept Nobel Prizes. Meanwhile, physicists have unofficially distributed some of the credit to Liese Meitner in Stockholm (a woman physicist) and R. Frisch of Copenhagen, who presented a fine interpretation of what happened when the uranium atom cracked. Some credit also went to Nobel Laureate Irene Curie-Joliot (daughter of Marie Curie) and P. Savitch of Paris, who had done work which helped Hahn identify the all-important barium in his bombardment products.

Since the first explosion reverberated through the world's laboratories, the fission of thorium, as well as uranium, has been demonstrated. Atom-wranglers at Columbia University have shown that, under various conditions, the fission of uranium yields krypton, strontium, iodine, xenon, tellurium as disintegration products. The flood of reports made it appear that atomic physicists are off on the biggest big-game hunt since the discovery of artificial radioactivity was announced in 1934.

Albert Einstein's famous letter follows. In overseeing its preparation, Leo Szilard had the collaboration of Eugene Wigner and Edward Teller, two of his fellow physicists who, like Szilard, were also originally from Hungary.

Source: Albert Einstein to F[ranklin] D. Roosevelt, August 2, 1939, President's Secretary's File: Safe File: Alexander Sachs, Franklin D. Roosevelt Library. Courtesy of Franklin D. Roosevelt Library, Hyde Park, New York.

Albert Einstein
Old Grove Rd.
Nassau Point
Peconic, Long Island

August 2nd, 1939

F.D. Roosevelt,
President of the United States,
White House
Washington, D.C.

Sir:

Some recent work by E.Fermi and L. Szilard, which has been communicated to me in manuscript, leads me to expect that the element uranium may be turned into a new and important source of energy in the immediate future. Certain aspects of the situation which has arisen seem to call for watchfulness and, if necessary, quick action on the part of the Administration. I believe therefore that it is my duty to bring to your attention the following facts and recommendations:

In the course of the last four months it has been made probable - through the work of Joliot in France as well as Fermi and Szilard in America - that it may become possible to set up a nuclear chain reaction in a large mass of uranium,by which vast amounts of power and large quantities of new radium-like elements would be generated. Now it appears almost certain that this could be achieved in the immediate future.

This new phenomenon would also lead to the construction of bombs, and it is conceivable - though much less certain - that extremely powerful bombs of a new type may thus be constructed. A single bomb of this type, carried by boat and exploded in a port, might very well destroy the whole port together with some of the surrounding territory. However, such bombs might very well prove to be too heavy for transportation by air.

The United States has only very poor ores of uranium in moderate quantities. There is some good ore in Canada and the former Czechoslovakia, while the most important source of uranium is Belgian Congo.

In view of this situation you may think it desirable to have some permanent contact maintained between the Administration and the group of physicists working on chain reactions in America. One possible way of achieving this might be for you to entrust with this task a person who has your confidence and who could perhaps serve in an inofficial capacity. His task might comprise the following:

a) to approach Government Departments, keep them informed of the further development, and put forward recommendations for Government action, giving particular attention to the problem of securing a supply of uranium ore for the United States;

b) to speed up the experimental work,which is at present being carried on within the limits of the budgets of University laboratories, by providing funds, if such funds be required, through his contacts with private persons who are willing to make contributions for this cause, and perhaps also by obtaining the co-operation of industrial laboratories which have the necessary equipment.

I understand that Germany has actually stopped the sale of uranium from the Czechoslovakian mines which she has taken over. That she should have taken such early action might perhaps be understood on the ground that the son of the German Under-Secretary of State, von Weizsäcker, is attached to the Kaiser-Wilhelm-Institut in Berlin where some of the American work on uranium is now being repeated.

Yours very truly,

A. Einstein

(Albert Einstein)

Assignment Reluctantly Accepted

When the Manhattan Engineer District—the MED—was just a few months old, Leslie R. Groves was chosen to succeed its first leader. Groves had the reputation of being able to move a big project along at the fastest possible pace, and he was put in place to do just that. He wrote a book about the Manhattan Project, published many years after the end of the war. This selection is from its early pages.

Source: Leslie R. Groves, *Now It Can Be Told: The Story of the Manhattan Project* (New York: Harper & Brothers, 1962), pp. 3-5. Copyright © 1962 by Leslie R. Groves. Reprinted by permission of Lieutenant General Richard H. Groves, Retired.

One day in mid-September, 1942, about a month and a half before the invasion of North Africa, I was offered an extremely attractive assignment overseas. At that time I had been on duty in Washington for over two years as Deputy Chief of Construction of the Army Corps of Engineers. Under the general supervision of my immediate superior, Major General T. M. Robins, I was in charge of all Army construction within the United States as well as in our off-shore bases. This included the building of camps, airfields, ordnance and chemical manufacturing plants, depots, port facilities and the like. But though the responsibility was great and the work essential, I was, like every other regular officer, extremely eager for service abroad as a commander of combat troops; and I now replied with deep pleasure that any duty in an active theater of operations appealed to me. However, I added, I would have to secure the consent of Lieutenant General Brehon Somervell, Commanding General of the Army Services of Supply, before I could definitely say yes. I promised to see him and to give my answer by noon the next day.

The following morning, a few minutes after I had finished testifying before a Congressional committee on a military housing bill, I met Somervell outside the hearing room, and asked him whether he had any objection to my being relieved from my Army construction duties. To my great surprise, he told me that I could not leave Washington. He went on to say: "The Secretary of War has selected you for a very important assignment, and the President has approved the selection."

"Where?"

"Washington."

"I don't want to stay in Washington."

"If you do the job right," Somervell said, "it will win the war."

My spirits fell as I realized what he had in mind. "Oh, that thing," I said. Somervell went on, "You can do it if it can be done. See [Major General W. D.] Styer . . . and he will give you the details."

My initial reaction was one of extreme disappointment. I did not know the details of America's atomic development program at that time, but, because of the nature of my responsibilities, as I shall explain, I knew of its existence and its general purpose—through the use of uranium to produce an atomic bomb which it was hoped might be of unprecedented power. Though a big project, it was not expected to involve as much as $100 million altogether. While this was more than the cost of almost any single job under my jurisdiction, it was much less than our total over-all spending in a normal week. . . . Magnitude aside, what little I knew of the project had not particularly impressed me, and if I had known the complete picture I would have been still less impressed.

Later that morning, I saw Styer at his office in the Pentagon. He confirmed my worst premonitions by telling me that I was to be placed in charge of the Army's part of the atomic effort. He outlined my mission, painting a very rosy picture for me: "The basic research and development are done. You just have to take the rough designs, put them into final shape, build some plants and organize an operating force and your job will be finished and the war will be over." Naturally I was skeptical, but it took me several weeks to realize just how overoptimistic an outlook he had presented.

. . . .

Before I left, Styer told me that [Army Chief of Staff] General [George C.] Marshall had directed that I be made a brigadier general, and that the list of new promotions would be out in a few days. I decided at once, and Styer agreed, that I should not take over the project officially until I could do so as a brigadier. I thought that there might be some problems in dealing with the many academic scientists involved in the project, and I felt that my position would be stronger if they thought of me from the first as a general instead of as a promoted colonel. My later experiences convinced me that this was a wise move; strangely enough, it often seemed to me that the prerogatives of rank were more important in the academic world than they are among soldiers.

. . . .

The First Self-Sustaining Chain Reaction

Early in 1942, the research that led to the first self-sustaining chain reaction was consolidated at the University of Chicago, in the Met Lab which was under the overall direction of the physicist Arthur Holly Compton. Along with his more senior colleague Enrico Fermi, Herbert L. Anderson moved to Chicago. Anderson was one of the fifty-two people present in a racquets court under the west stands of Stagg Field, the university's football stadium, when the research came to fruition on December 2, 1942. The following selection is drawn from a longer paper he prepared for a symposium commemorating the occasion's fortieth anniversary.

Source: Herbert L. Anderson, "The First Chain Reaction" in *The Nuclear Chain Reaction—Forty Years Later*, ed. Robert G. Sachs ([Chicago:] The University of Chicago, 1984), pp. 35, 37. Copyright © 1984 by The University of Chicago. Reprinted by permission of The University of Chicago.

· ·

As it happened, on December 2, a group from DuPont arrived in Chicago, as part of a review they were conducting, to see where they could do the most good among the various activities of the Manhattan District. When they arrived Compton told them that Fermi was about to carry out his test of the first chain reaction. There were quite a few people already there. It was getting kind of crowded. There were the people who put it together and there were others who wanted to be present and had enough clout to get in. . . . The DuPont group was invited to select one of their number to witness the performance. They chose Crawford Greenewalt. It was quite a show! I had very little to do at that time. Fermi was in charge. He soon began to issue instructions to George Weil who was down on the floor where he could manipulate one of the cadmium control rods.

To register the neutron intensity, we had a boron-trifluoride counter. It was connected to a scalar which operated a mechanical counter. The counter made a loud sound every time it registered a count. It went clack! And after the next 16 pulses from the boron-trifluoride counter, it would go clack again. Just by listening you could tell what the neutron intensity was.

When he began all the control rods were in the pile. Fermi ordered all removed except the one operated by George Weil. He then asked George to pull that rod out a foot. Fermi recorded the activity as indicated by the counter, so many clacks per minute. The rod was pulled out another foot and a new measurement was made. Fermi would put each measurement on a graph and then, with a little slide rule, he would calculate where the next point ought to go. He had done his homework and knew what to expect. Each data point was analyzed on the spot.

These preliminary measurements went on for a while and in due course it became lunch time. It was Fermi's habit to go to lunch at noon and this occasion was no exception. It wasn't a good idea to do an important experiment on an empty stomach.

The serious work began after lunch. Fermi had calculated that the system would become critical by removing 8 feet of the cadmium strip. He called for the strip to be pulled one foot at a time. The increase in intensity was obvious to everyone on the balcony. You could hear those clacks and each time the strip was removed further the clacks came faster and faster. At each step Fermi would record the result, make a calculation, and announce something like, "The next time we pull out the strip by one foot, the rate will go from 600 to 1200 a minute." Then the rod would be pulled out and everybody could tell by the sound that the predictions were in the right ball park. They weren't exactly on but each time he got closer. You got the feeling that Fermi really knew what he was doing, that he had everything under control.

At a certain point he announced that by pulling out the cadmium strip a final foot and one-half, the pile would go critical. Instead of leveling off as had been the case before, the intensity would continue to rise indefinitely in an exponential fashion.

The rod was pulled out the specified amount and you could hear the counters clicking away—clickety-clack, clackity-click. They went faster and faster and then at a certain point suddenly there was silence. The rate had become too great for the counters to follow. It was a dramatic moment. An important threshold had been passed. Attention turned to the chart recorder. It was silent but could record much higher levels of intensity. You watched a pen moving across the scale as the chart advanced....

The intensity kept rising and soon the pen was off-scale. So the scale was changed, the pen returned to a point near zero and then began to move across the scale again. The rise in intensity was exponential as the record shows. After a change in scale by a factor of 10, it was understandable that some of the onlookers might become a little nervous. They didn't hear anything, they didn't feel anything, but they knew that a dangerous acitivity was mounting rapidly. Everyone's eyes were on Fermi. It was up to him to call a halt. But he was very confident and very calm. He wanted the intensity to rise high enough to remove all possible doubt that the pile was critical. He kept it going until it seemed too much to bear. "Zip in," he called, and Zinn released his rope.† The control rod he held went in with a bang and the intensity dropped abruptly to comfortable levels. Everyone sighed with relief. Then there was a small cheer. The experiment was a success.

† "Zip" was the name given to one special control rod. Ed.

One Glimpse of Life at Los Alamos

Many scientists brought their families with them to Los Alamos so that it became not just an Army base housing a weapons laboratory but a community in a broader sense. One of its residents was Enrico Fermi's observant, literate, and witty wife, Laura. This selection contains some of her recollections about life on the Hill.

Source: Laura Fermi, *Atoms in the Family: My Life with Enrico Fermi* (Chicago: The University of Chicago Press, 1954), pp. 226-29. Copyright © 1954 by The University of Chicago. Reprinted by permission of The University of Chicago Press.

All ellipses in this selection are in the original text except the one in line 2 on page 28, following "personnel."

There are several ways of expressing the same concept. In his official report on atomic energy Mr. [Henry DeWolf] Smyth asserts that ". . .the end of 1944 found an extraordinary galaxy of scientific stars gathered on this New Mexican Mesa."

At about the time which Mr. Smyth refers to, General Groves summoned all Army officers stationed in Los Alamos and gave them a talk. The story goes that he opened his speech with the sentence: "At great expense we have gathered on this mesa the largest collection of crackpots ever seen." The "crackpots" were dear to the General, who went on recommending them to the good care of his officers.

A third way of stating the same idea is to say that Los Alamos was all one big family and all one big accent; that everybody in science was there, both from the United States and from almost all the European countries.

An intellectual *émigré* is a person selected by certain special traits of intelligence, initiative, adaptability, and spirit of adventure. Facts seem to prove that when these traits join those

25

common to most scientists, they produce queer persons indeed. Hence General Groves's choice of the word "crackpots," which, we felt, applied especially to the numerous European-born men of science on the mesa.

"But I am an exception," Enrico said after relating to me General Groves's alleged speech. "I am perfectly normal."

We had just finished lunch, and Enrico was preparing to return to work. He rolled up his pants, straddled his bicycle, waved goodbye, and started up the steep street. In the effort to pedal uphill, he let the belt of his sport jacket ride halfway up his stooping back. His shrunken blue-cloth hat, which he wore steadily both in rain and in shine, was perched precariously on top of his head. I wondered...normal...perfectly normal....

Four minutes later I heard the one o'clock siren. At that precise moment Enrico would disembark from his bicycle in front of the Tech Area gate and would show his white badge to the guard. Enrico is never late, not even in the morning.

The first siren of the day went off at 7:00 A.M. It warned that work would start in an hour. Then Enrico stretched out in his bed, yawned, and remarked:

"Oppie has whistled. It is time to get up." Oppie was the director of the laboratories. If the sirens went off, it *must* be Oppie's doing.

In early morning there was a scramble in the house. The children were to get ready for school; Enrico took too long to shave in the bathroom which had no bath, but only a shower. Protests...shouts...a "Now it's my turn," in a shrill boyish voice..., an "I am older, I'll go first." An occasional fight.... Some unavoidable kicking under the breakfast table if the children sat across from each other; some work of the fists if they sat side by side.

Then the house was suddenly still. I did the dishes, started a soup that would be cooking all morning on the GI electric plate, and by nine I was at work in the Tech Area.

At that period wives were encouraged to work. There was great scarcity of clerical help at first, and some young men had been asked to join the Los Alamos group both because they were good physicists and because their wives were experienced secretaries. Harold Agnew, the student who had helped move the small pile from Columbia University, was of the number: Oppie had considered Beverley Agnew an additional asset and had hired both.

Apart from the shortage of woman power, which slowly decreased as single girls joined the project, it was an established policy to encourage wives to work. Colonel Stafford Warren, the head of the Health Division of the Manhattan District, placed little faith in women's moral fortitude. In the early days of the project he declared himself in favor of giving work to the wives to "keep them out of mischief."

The wives were only too happy for an opportunity to peek inside secret places, to share the war effort, to earn a bit of money. I worked three hours, six mornings a week, as clerical assistant to the doctor's secretary in the Tech Area. I was classified in the lowest category of employees, for I had no special experience or a college degree. When Enrico had asked me to marry him, I was halfway through school, and there seemed to be no point in waiting until I finished. Few married women had a career in Italy at that period, unless there was real need for more earnings in the family.

So in Los Alamos I was paid at the lowest rate for my three daily hours, which was not much; but I was kept busy, happy, and "out of mischief." I was given a blue badge that admitted me to the Tech Area but did not permit that I be told

27

secrets; these were all saved for the white badges, the technical personnel. . . .

. . . .

My work kept me well informed about all sorts of inconsequential details. I knew who had a bad cold and whose splitting headache was relieved by aspirin from our office. Because I had been classified so low, my tasks were confined to preparing, filing, and bringing up to date personnel cards. I could also mark medical histories "secret" in red with a rubber stamp. I was acquainted with the number of corpuscles in many people's blood, and I learned immediately if a man had been transferred from one part of the project to another.

I passed on my information to Enrico, who never knew anything. He was associate director of the laboratories, but, to my great amusement, I was always the first to tell him the gossip of the Tech Area and the personnel movements.

Besides being associate director, Enrico was the leader of the "F Division," in which F stood for Fermi. When he arrived at Los Alamos, he managed to gather a group of very brilliant men. One of them was his imaginative friend Edward Teller; another was Herbert Anderson, Enrico's inseparable collaborator. No specific assignment was given to the F Division, but they solved a number of problems which did not fit in the work of any other division. It was typical of Enrico to be engrossed in his work and to pay no attention to what was going on around him.

. . . .

Trinity

William L. Laurence was a veteran science reporter for The New York Times. *Before a veil of secrecy descended, he had closely covered early developments about fission. Even after the subject went underground, his reporter's faculties gleaned him at least a sketchy sense about the dramatic things happening in Tennessee, Washington, and New Mexico, but nothing too precise. Then in the spring of 1945, General Groves approached him. He asked Laurence to join the project to handle a number of its important writing assignments in anticipation of the time, then rapidly approaching, when the huge undertaking would become public knowledge. Laurence got to visit the secret facilities around Clinton and Hanford as well as those at Los Alamos. And he was the only reporter present in the New Mexican desert for Trinity. This account tells of that experience.*

Source: William L. Laurence, *Men and Atoms: The Discovery, the Uses and the Future of Atomic Energy* (New York: Simon and Schuster, 1959), pp. 115-18. Copyright © 1959 by William L. Laurence. Copyright renewed © 1987 by Mrs. Florence D. Laurence. Reprinted by permission of Simon & Schuster, Inc.

I watched the birth of the atomic age from the slope of a hill in the desert land of New Mexico, on the northwestern corner of the Alamogordo Air Base, about 125 miles southeast of Albuquerque. The hill, named Compania Hill for the occasion, was twenty miles to the northwest of Zero, the code name given to the spot chosen for the atomic-bomb test. The area embracing Zero and Compania Hill, twenty-four miles long and eighteen miles wide, bore the code name Trinity.

The bomb was set on a structural steel tower one hundred feet high. Ten miles away to the southwest was the base camp. This was G.H.Q. for the scientific high command, of which

Professor Kenneth T. Bainbridge of Harvard University was field commander. Here were erected barracks to serve as living quarters for the scientists, a mess hall, a commissary, a post exchange, and other buildings. The vanguard of the scientists, headed by Dr. Oppenheimer, lived like soldiers at the front, supervising the enormously complicated details of the test.

Here early that Sunday afternoon had gathered General Groves; Brigadier-General Thomas F. Farrell, hero of World War I, General Groves's deputy; Dr. Fermi; Dr. Conant; Dr. Bush; Professor Robert F. Bacher of Cornell; Colonel Stafford L. Warren, University of Rochester radiologist; and about 150 other leaders in the atomic-bomb project.

At the base camp was a dry, abandoned reservoir, about five hundred feet square, surrounded by a mound of earth about eight feet high. Within this mound bulldozers dug a series of slit trenches, each about three feet deep, seven feet wide and twenty-five feet long. At a command over the radio at zero minus one minute all observers at base camp were to lie down in their assigned trenches, "face and eyes directed toward the ground and with the head away from Zero." But most of us on Compania Hill remained on our feet.

At our observation post on Compania Hill the atmosphere had grown tenser as the zero hour approached. We had spent the first part of our stay eating an early-morning picnic breakfast. It had grown cold in the desert, and many of us, lightly clad, shivered. Occasionally a drizzle came down, and the intermittent flashes of lightning made us glance apprehensively toward Zero. We had received some disturbing reports that the test might be called off because of the weather. The radio we had brought with us for communication with base camp kept going out of order, and when we finally repaired it some noisy band would drown out the news we wanted to hear. We knew there were two specially equipped B-29 Superfortresses high overhead to make observations and recordings in the upper atmosphere, but we could neither see nor hear them. We kept gazing through the blackness.

Suddenly, at 5:29:50, as we stood huddled around our radio, we heard a voice ringing through the darkness, sounding as though it had come from above the clouds: "Zero minus ten seconds!" † A green flare flashed out through the clouds, descended slowly, opened, grew dim, and vanished into the darkness.

† Across sources, there is some minor variation in the time identified as the exact moment of detonation. Ed.

Physicist and Navy officer Norris E. Bradbury atop the tower at Ground Zero with the atomic device—the "gadget," as it was typically called in-house. After the war, Bradbury would succeed Oppenheimer as director of the laboratory at Los Alamos.

The voice from the clouds boomed out again: "Zero minus three seconds!" Another green flare came down. Silence reigned over the desert. We kept moving in small groups in the direction of Zero. From the east came the first faint signs of dawn.

And just at that instant there rose as if from the bowels of the earth a light not of this world, the light of many suns in one. It was a sunrise such as the world had never seen, a great green supersun climbing in a fraction of a second to a height of more than eight thousand feet, rising ever higher until it touched the clouds, lighting up earth and sky all around with a dazzling luminosity.

Up it went, a great ball of fire about a mile in diameter, changing colors as it kept shooting upward, from deep purple to orange, expanding, growing bigger, rising as it expanded, an elemental force freed from its bonds after being chained for billions of years. For a fleeting instant the color was unearthly green, such as one sees only in the corona of the sun during a total eclipse. It was as though the earth had opened and the skies had split.

A huge cloud rose from the ground and followed the trail of the great sun. At first it was a giant column, which soon took the shape of a supramundane mushroom. Up it went, higher and higher, quivering convulsively, a giant mountain born in a few seconds instead of millions of years. It touched the multi-colored clouds, pushed its summit through them, and kept rising until it reached a height of 41,000 feet, 12,000 feet higher than the earth's highest mountain.

All through the very short but long-seeming time interval not a sound was heard. I could see the silhouettes of human forms motionless in little groups, like desert plants in the dark. The newborn mountain in the distance, a giant among the pygmies of the Sierra Oscuro range, stood leaning at an angle against the clouds, like a vibrant volcano spouting fire to the sky.

Then out of the great silence came a mighty thunder. For a brief interval the phenomena we had seen as light repeated themselves in terms of sound. It was the blast from thousands of blockbusters going off simultaneously at one spot. The thunder reverberated all through the desert, bounced back and forth from the Sierra Oscuro, echo upon echo. The ground trembled under our feet as in an earthquake. A wave of hot wind was felt by many of us just before the blast and warned us of its coming.

The big boom came about a hundred seconds after the great flash—the first cry of a newborn world.

It brought the silent, motionless silhouettes to life, gave them a voice. A loud cry filled the air. The little groups that had hitherto stood rooted to the earth like desert plants broke into a dance—the rhythm of primitive man dancing at one of his fire festivals at the coming of spring.

They clapped their hands as they leaped from the ground—earthbound man symbolizing the birth of a new force that gives him means to free himself from the gravitational bonds that hold him down.

The dance of the primitive man lasted but a few seconds, during which an evolutionary period of 10,000 years had been telescoped. Primitive man was metamorphosed in those few seconds into modern man.

The sun was just rising above the horizon as our caravan started on its way back to Albuquerque and Los Alamos. We looked at it through our dark lenses to compare it with what we had seen.

"The sun can't hold a candle to it!" one of us remarked.

On arriving at Los Alamos I called on Dr. Oppenheimer. He looked tired and preoccupied. I asked him how he felt at the moment of the flash.

"At that moment," I heard him say, "there flashed into my mind a passage from the Bhagavad-Gita, the sacred book of the Hindus: 'I am become Death, the Shatterer of Worlds!'"

I shall never forget the shattering impact of those words, spoken by a poet and a dreamer, one of the most civilized of men, called upon by destiny to direct the harnessing of one of the supreme achievements of man's intellect onto the chariot of Death.

Later that Monday morning, at the breakfast table in the pleasant dining room of the Los Alamos Lodge, the silence was broken by Dr. George B. Kistiakowsky of Harvard. Though he was seated next to me, his voice seemed to come from a great distance. And what I heard has been haunting me ever since.

"This was the nearest to doomsday one can possibly imagine," he said. "I am sure," he added after a pause, as though speaking to no one in particular, "that at the end of the world—in the last millisecond of the earth's existence—the last man—will see something very similar to what we have seen."

And out of the silence that ensued I heard another voice—my own—which also sounded as though it came from a distance.

"Possibly so," I said, "but it is also possible that if the first man could have been present at the moment of Creation when God said, 'Let there be light,' he might have seen something very similar to what we have seen."

. . . .

Enrico Fermi prepared the following report about Trinity which remained classified until into 1983. He made an estimate of the blast's magnitude which is impressive for both the simplicity of its method and its accuracy. His estimate diverged by less than a factor of two from another estimate, based on more sophisticated procedures, which indicated that Trinity's blast was equivalent to one from 18,600 tons of TNT.

Source: E[nrico] Fermi, "My Observations During the Explosion at Trinity on July 16, 1945," Collection VFA-470, 1945, Los Alamos National Laboratory Archives. Courtesy of Los Alamos National Laboratory, Los Alamos, New Mexico.

My Observations During the Explosion at Trinity on July 16, 1945 — E. Fermi

On the morning of the 16th of July, I was stationed at the Base Camp at Trinity in a position about ten miles from the site of the explosion.

The explosion took place at about 5:30 A.M. I had my face protected by a large board in which a piece of dark welding glass had been inserted. My first impression of the explosion was the very intense flash of light, and a sensation of heat on the parts of my body that were exposed. Although I did not look directly towards the object, I had the impression that suddenly the countryside became brighter than in full daylight. I subsequently looked in the direction of the explosion through the dark glass and could see something that looked like a conglomeration of flames that promptly started rising. After a few seconds the rising flames lost their brightness and appeared as a huge pillar of smoke with an expanded head like a gigantic mushroom that rose rapidly beyond the clouds probably to a height of the order of 30,000 feet. After reaching its full height, the smoke stayed stationary for a while before the wind started dispersing it.

About 40 seconds after the explosion the air blast reached me. I tried to estimate its strength by dropping from about six feet small pieces of paper before, during and after the passage of the blast wave. Since at the time, there was no wind I could observe very distinctly and actually measure the displacement of the pieces of paper that were in the process of falling while the blast was passing. The shift was about 2½ meters, which, at the time, I estimated to correspond to the blast that would be produced by ten thousand tons of T.N.T.

UNCLASSIFIED

Munitions Explode at Alamo Dump

(By The Associated Press)

An ammunition magazine exploded early today in a remote area of the Alamogordo Air Base reservation, producing a brilliant flash and blast which were reported to have been observed as far away as Gallup, 235 miles northwest.

Col. William O. Eareckson, Alamogordo commandant, declared there was "no loss of life or injury to anyone, and that property damage outside of the explosives magazine itself were negligible."

His statement said the magazine contained "a considerable amount of high explosives and pyrotechnics," and that "weather conditions affecting the content of gas shells exploded by the blast" might make it desirable to evacuate temporarily a few civilians.

There is a civilian area on the reservation.

At Alamogordo, 10 miles from the base, Mrs. Tom Charles said she knew of no damage there from the explosion.

At Silver City, 135 miles southwest, and at Gallup the blast rattled windows. The vivid flash preceding the concussion by several minutes was reported seen near Silver City, Gallup, and on highways around Albuquerque, 150 miles north.

"I saw a flash of fire followed by a violent explosion and smoke," reported Ranger Kay Smith on duty on the Lookout Mountain tower, near Beaverhead, northwest of Silver City.

He said there were two other smaller explosions, occurring at 5:30 a. m. He said he had no explanation for the blasts.

From Gallup came reports that two explosions rattled windows there this morning and awoke a number of persons at 5:45 a. m.

An explosion heard near Socorro "lighted up the sky like the sun," reported Joe Wills, Socorro theater operator.

The Army had gotten ready in advance to issue a phony press release following Trinity if such camouflage became necessary. As things worked out, it did. The Albuquerque Tribune *was an afternoon newspaper. On July 16, 1945, not too many hours after the successful experiment in the desert, it ran the adjacent article. The story was also covered elsewhere in New Mexico and beyond. But the real story remained a closely guarded secret for three more weeks.*

The tower at Ground Zero

Hiroshima

Colonel Paul W. Tibbets, Jr., was certainly one of the Air Force's most skillful bomber pilots, maybe its best. In September of 1944, he had been put in command of the unit that became the 509th Composite Group. Its assignment was to develop the capability to deliver the atomic bomb to a target. The B-29 was an advanced aircraft of the day, and the unit had access to many of them. By mid-June of 1945, the 509th had begun assembling on the Pacific island of Tinian. From there it would launch its strikes. When the Enola Gay, *the plane carrying* Little Boy, *took off to bomb Hiroshima, Tibbets was its pilot. Here is his account, originally published less than a year after the event.*

Source: Col. Paul W. Tibbe[t]s, Jr., as told to Wesley Price, "How to Drop an Atom Bomb," *The Saturday Evening Post*, June 8, 1946, pp. 135-36.† Reprinted from *The Saturday Evening Post*, copyright © 1946. Reprinted by permission.

† "Tibbets" is correct. In the magazine, it was incorrectly spelled "Tibbetts."

. . . .

When we came to Tinian, at long last, we had all the training we could absorb, and the best of equipment. My orders had been to organize a sort of 1st Individual Air Force, which could go anywhere in the world and operate without support.

So the 509th Composite Group had its own troop-carrier squadron, its own control-tower personnel, its own engineering squadron.

We could make repairs of such complexity that they almost amounted to rebuilding a plane; and, given time, we could build our own airfield. We had our own military police guarding our own reserved corner at North Field. We had better, newer and shinier tools than anyone else on the island and—prized possession!—we had a supersonic radar trainer.

This was the way we set ourselves to drop atom bombs. If it would have helped, we would have worn solid-gold uniforms with pearl buttons. But, just as we were, we weren't winning friends. Veteran fliers who'd been commuting from Tinian to Japan with fire bombs asked loudly, "Why all the secrecy? Why the plush? Are we living on the wrong side of the railroad tracks?"

Our test missions were secret. When a 509th plane took off, no one knew its destination except Maj. Gen. Curtis LeMay† and us. Sometimes we dropped facsimiles of the atom bomb at sea. Sometimes a single B-29 flew to Japan and dropped one demolition bomb very accurately. We didn't say. Secret report to General LeMay. Top-secret strike photos, for General LeMay only. An exasperated clerk in base operations jabbed at us in verse:

NOBODY KNOWS

Into the air the secret rose,
Where they're going nobody knows;
Tomorrow they'll return again,
But we'll never know where they've been.
Don't ask about results or such,
Unless you want to get in Dutch;
But take it from one who is sure of the score,
The 509th is winning the war.

When the other Groups are ready to go,
We have a program of the whole damned show;
And when Halsey's Fifth shells Nippon's shore,
Why, shucks, we hear about it the day before;
And MacArthur and Doolittle give it out in advance,

---

† The spelling used in the magazine, "Le May," has been corrected here to "LeMay." Ed.

But with this new bunch we haven't a chance.
We should have been home a month or more,
For the 509th is winning the war.

Every bombardier in the group could draw from memory a map of the approaches to the Japanese coast and the target areas. On August fifth, crews were shown photographs of the test explosion in New Mexico.

Antiglare goggles were issued, but the true nature of the bomb was not revealed.

By dinnertime of the fifth, all briefing was completed. The atom bomb was ready, the planes were gassed and checked. Take-off was set for 2:30 A.M.

I tried to nap, but visitors kept me up. Dutch swallowed two sleeping tablets, then sat up wide awake all night playing poker with Beahan, Ferebee and Sweeney. At 1:00 A.M. we had ham and eggs. At 1:30 A.M., three of our planes took off to scout targets in Japan for weather.

The atom bomb was tucked into my plane, Enola Gay. I had Bob Lewis as copilot, Dutch Van Kirk as navigator, and Ferebee as bombardier. Two B-29's were going with us. Chuck Sweeney had one carrying gauges to measure the force of the blast. George Marquardt had the photo plane.

We started engines at 2:15 A.M. It was just another mission, if you didn't let imagination run away with your wits.

I forgot the atom bomb and concentrated on the cockpit check.

I called the tower, "Dimples Eight Two to North Tinian Tower. Taxi-out and take-off instructions."

"Dimples Eight Two from North Tinian Tower. Take-off to the east on Runway A for Able."

At the end of the runway, another call to the tower and a quick response: "Dimples Eight Two cleared for take-off."

Bob Lewis called off the time. Fifteen seconds to go. Ten seconds. Five seconds. Get ready ———

I eased the brakes at exactly 2:30 A.M. Dimples Eight Two took off for Japan and the Atomic Age.

At cruising altitude I drank some coffee, then crawled back to tell the crew about that thing in the bomb bay.

They listened, understood and remained calm. An atom bomb. Check.

At 8:15 A.M. Pfc. Richard N. Nelson, our radio operator, received signals from the weather scouts. Two targets had slight cloud cover. But Maj. Claude Eatherly was reporting ten miles' visibility over Hiroshima, with light haze. We continued the climb, three B-29's in loose formation.

We started the bomb run by radar twenty-five miles from Hiroshima. Our altitude was 30,000 feet indicated, 31,600 feet true, and we would drop exactly according to plan, at 9:15 A.M.†

Twelve miles from the target, Ferebee called, "I see it!"

He clutched in his bombsight and took control of the plane from me for a visual run. Dutch kept giving me radar course corrections. He was working with the radar operator, S/Sgt. Joseph A. Stiborik. I couldn't raise them on the interphone to tell them Ferebee had the plane.

Ferebee had the drift well killed, but the rate was off a little. He made two slight corrections. A loud "blip" on the radio notified the escort B-29's that the bomb would drop in two minutes. After that, Tom looked up from his bombsight once and nodded to me; it was going to be okay.

He motioned to the radio operator to give the final warning. A continuous tone signal went out, telling Sweeney and Marquardt: "In fifteen seconds she goes."

† At 9:15 A.M. on the *Enola Gay*, it was 8:15 A.M. in Hiroshima. Ed.

The radio tone ended, the bomb dropped, Ferebee unclutched his sight, I threw off the automatic pilot and hauled Enola Gay into the turn.

I pulled antiglare goggles over my eyes. I couldn't see through them; I was blind. I threw them to the floor.

A bright light filled the plane. The first shock wave hit us.

We were eleven and a half miles slant range from the atomic explosion, but the whole airplane cracked and crinkled from the blast. I yelled "Flak!" thinking a heavy gun battery had found us.

The tail gunner had seen the first wave coming, a visible shimmer in the atmosphere, but he didn't know what it was until it hit. When the second wave came, he called out a warning.

We turned back to look at Hiroshima. The city was hidden by that awful cloud which everyone has seen in photographs, boiling up, mushrooming, terrible and incredibly tall.

No one spoke for a moment; then everyone was talking. I remember Lewis pounding my shoulder, saying, "Look at that! Look at that! Look at that!" Tom Ferebee wondered aloud whether radioactivity would make us all sterile. Lewis said he could taste atomic fission. He said it tasted like lead.

Ferebee radioed a strike report to Tinian. "Results good." Our naval observer, Capt. William S. Parsons—now an admiral —filed another report en route home: "Results excellent."

"Good hell," he said, "What did you expect? It was perfect."

We hadn't seen the newspaper headlines, we'd only seen the atomic explosion, so we didn't know how big it was. When we landed, someone yelled, "Attention!" and Gen. Tooey Spaatz came forward. He pinned the D.S.C. [Distinguished Service Cross] on me while I stood at attention, palming the bowl of my pipe and trying to work the stem up my sleeve.

The next day I was taken into the war room at Guam to meet the correspondents. I'd never seen so many in one place. They looked at me queerly. Nobody spoke for a minute. Then they asked questions, and the atom bomb was bigger than the cloud we had seen over Hiroshima.

"How did you feel?" they asked. There would be other questions, but they'd come back to it again and again. "How did you feel?"

I told them about the 509th Composite Group, and how proud I was of it, but that wasn't what they meant.

People still ask me: "How did you feel?" I might answer with a question: "How do you feel?" We're all living in the Atomic Age together, and the atom bomb was made and dropped for the people of the United States.

The End

Nagasaki

Trinity was not the only atomic explosion William L. Laurence witnessed in the summer of 1945. (See pages 29-34.) Without initially knowing his destination, he was dispatched to Tinian. Because of delays in transit, he arrived too late to go along on the bombing of Hiroshima. But three days after the first mission to drop an atomic bomb, there was a second, and he was on that one. Nagasaki became its target. Here is Laurence's chronicle.

Source: William L. Laurence, *Men and Atoms: The Discovery, the Uses and the Future of Atomic Energy* (New York: Simon and Schuster, 1959), pp. 154-61. Copyright © 1959 by William L. Laurence. Copyright renewed © 1987 by Mrs. Florence D. Laurence. Reprinted by permission of Simon & Schuster, Inc.

The ellipsis in the last line on page 47 is Laurence's punctuation; it does not signify a deletion by the editor.

· ·

I climbed into the nose of the B-29, the instrument plane which was to follow directly behind the strike plane, No. 77. The quarters were cramped and the only place I could find to sit was a hard metal box. The pilot of my ship was Captain Frederick C. Bock, of Greenville, Michigan . . . . The night outside was dark and uncertain.

It was 3:50 Thursday morning, August 9, when I became airborne. Seated on the metal box, I took out a small notebook and began writing a play-by-play account . . . . The dateline read: "With the Atomic Bomb Mission to Japan, Thursday, August 9." It was the first and only dateline of its kind in history.

The paragraph read:

We are on our way to bomb the homeland of Japan, in a formation equivalent to 2,000, and possibly 4,000, B-29 Superbombers. Actually our flying contingent consists of only three specially designed B-29s, and two of them carry no bombs. But our lead plane, about 3,000 feet directly ahead, is on its way with another atomic bomb, the second in three days, concentrating in its active substance an explosive energy equivalent to 20,000, and under favorable conditions 40,000, tons of TNT.

. . . The weather report had predicted storms ahead part of the way, but clear weather for the final stages. The storm broke just about one hour after we had left Tinian.

On we went . . . . We rode out the storm. On and on we went on a straight course to the Empire. The first signs of dawn came shortly after five o'clock. By 5:50 it was light outside.

The bombardier, First Lieutenant Charles Levy of Philadelphia, came over and offered me his front-row seat in the transparent nose of the ship. From that vantage point in space, 17,000 feet above the Pacific, I could see hundreds of miles on all sides, horizontally and vertically. At that height the ocean below and the sky above appear to merge into one great sphere.

. . . .

At 9:12 we reached Yakoshima, our assembly point, a little island southeast of Kyushu, and there, about four thousand feet ahead of us, was No. 77 with its atomic load. I saw Lieutenant Leonard A. Godfrey of Greenfield, Massachusetts, the navigator, and Sergeant Ralph D. Curry of Hoopeston, Illinois, the radio operator, strap on their parachutes, and I did likewise.

. . . .

From the time we reached Yakoshima fate started playing a grim game with us. Our troubles started when the third plane in our group, which was to make the official photographs of the bombing, did not join us within the expected time limit. We circled and circled, endlessly it seemed, around the little island. More than forty-five minutes had passed when the lead ship decided not to wait any longer.

It was 9:56 when we began heading for the coast line. The weather planes, half an hour ahead of us, had signaled good visibility over Kokura as well as Nagasaki. But our arrival over Kokura had been delayed by more than three quarters of an hour, and when we got there the weather had changed and thick clouds covered the target. We had located the city by radar, but the orders were to make only a visual drop, which has the advantage of greater accuracy. This meant circling until we found an opening through the clouds over the selected target area. But the winds of destiny decreed otherwise.

Round . . . in wide circles went No. 77. Round and round went our ship close behind. But Kokura remained hidden . . . .

What was at stake was the ending of the war as quickly as possible. Turning back for another try the following morning might mean prolonging the war by at least one day, and every day the war went on meant the loss of many lives. And too much time had passed since the weather plane's report on the visibility over Nagasaki. The chances were therefore about even that it was by then no better than over Kokura.

We were making our third run over Kokura and had flown over Japan for about two hours when I suddenly saw large black rings come shooting through the white sea of clouds. I watched them in a dreamlike state of semiawareness, seeing them come higher and nearer, yet in no way realizing what they meant.

Suddenly, I came to. "That's flak!" I exclaimed. "The Japs are shooting at us!"

I counted fifteen black rings in rapid succession, all too low. Eight more followed, right up to our altitude, but too far to the left.

I began fingering the ring of my parachute. Would I ever make it? I had never made a parachute jump and at that time we were flying over water at an altitude of more than thirty thousand feet.

I was by far the oldest man in the plane and I knew that my chances of making a safe landing in the water, or of surviving even if I did make a landing, were certainly not as good as they would be for the young crew members in the prime of life.

I turned to Sergeant Curry, the twenty-year-old radio operator. I showed him the notebook in which the story . . . up to that moment had already been scribbled down by me in pencil.

"If we have to jump," I said, "would you be good enough to take this notebook? Give it to the first American officer you see as soon as you get back to an American camp and tell him it's the story of the mission over Kokura and Nagasaki up to the minute we were forced to bail out."

"Don't worry," Sergeant Curry said, apparently less concerned than I was.

On leaving Washington I had been given an impressive-looking official card, bearing my fingerprints and photograph, which stated that I was the bearer of the rank of "simulated colonel," entitling me to all the privileges of a full colonel. But stamped across the card in bold red letters was the line, "Valid only if captured by the enemy."

What a helluva way to become a colonel, I said to myself as I caressed the ring of my parachute. I could see myself waving the card as I landed and proclaiming to the enemy, "Here comes Colonel Laurence!"

As the black rings came ever nearer, as it seemed, I said to myself, Any minute now you may become a colonel!

Just after we had got out of the range of the flak, we noticed a squadron of Japanese fighter planes emerging from the clouds, spiraling upward toward us. The approach of the fighter planes and the flak from Kokura finally forced the pilot of the strike plane to change course. Destiny had chosen Nagasaki.

A careful check on the fuel supply revealed that No. 77, which started 700 gallons short (no one knows how this shortage came about), had enough fuel left for only one run on the target, and that if the bomb were not dropped, thus lightening the load, there would not be enough fuel to reach our emergency landing field at Okinawa.

We flew southward down the channel and at 11:33 crossed the coast line and headed straight for Nagasaki, about 100 miles to the west. And the nearer we came the greater grew our dejection. Nagasaki too was hidden under a curtain of clouds.

Would we drop the bomb by radar if we could not find an opening on the first and only possible run, and thus risk being off the mark, or would we continue looking for an opening until we had only enough gas left to reach our naval rescue craft in Japanese waters? Maybe we would go even farther—keep on looking for an opening until the last drop and then bail out over enemy territory. What were the misfortunes, or lives, of a handful of men in two B-29s against the chance of shortening the war?

It was up to the pilot and the weaponeer to make the decision, and they would have to make it fast. In the aircraft ahead of us two men were just then weighing our fate, and their own, in the balance.

We were then approaching the end of the first run. In a few minutes we would know the answer. The clouds below were still as impenetrable as ever.

And then, at the very last minute, there came an opening. For a few brief moments Nagasaki stood out clearly in broad noontime daylight.

Our watches stood at noon. The seconds ticked away. One, two, three. Ten, twenty, thirty, forty. Fifty. Fifty-seven, fifty-eight, fifty-nine...

It was 12:01 over Nagasaki.†

We heard the prearranged signal on our radio, put on our arc welder's glasses and watched tensely the maneuverings of the strike ship about half a mile in front of us.

"There she goes!" someone said.

Out of the belly of No. 77 a black object went downward.

Our B-29 swung around to get out of range; but even though we were turning away in the opposite direction, and despite the fact that it was broad daylight in our cabin, all of us became aware of a giant flash that broke through the dark barrier of our arc welder's lenses and flooded our cabin with intense light.

After the first flash we removed our glasses, but the light lingered on, a bluish-green light that illuminated the entire sky all around. A tremendous blast wave struck our ship and made it tremble from nose to tail. This was followed by four more blasts in rapid succession, each resounding like the boom of cannon hitting our plane from all directions.

Observers in the tail of our ship saw a giant ball of fire rise as though from the bowels of the earth, belching forth enormous white smoke rings. Next they saw a giant pillar of purple fire, ten thousand feet high, shooting skyward with enormous speed.

By the time our ship had made another turn in the direction of the atomic explosion the pillar of purple fire had reached the level of our altitude. Only about forty-five seconds had passed.

Awestruck, we watched it shoot upward like a meteor coming from the earth instead of from outer space, becoming ever more alive as it climbed skyward through the white clouds. It was no longer smoke, or dust, or even a cloud of fire. It was a living thing, a new species of being, born right before our eyes.

At one stage of its evolution, covering millions of years in terms of seconds, the entity assumed the form of a giant square

† In Nagasaki, the time was an hour earlier than on the airplane. Ed.

totem pole, with its base about three miles long, tapering off to about a mile at the top. Its bottom was brown, its center amber, its top white.

Then, just when it appeared as though the thing had settled down into a state of permanence, there came shooting out of the top a giant mushroom that increased the height of the pillar to a total of 45,000 feet.

The mushroom top was even more alive than the pillar, seething and boiling in a white fury of creamy foam, sizzling upward and then descending earthward, a thousand geysers rolled into one.

It kept struggling in an elemental fury, like a creature in the act of breaking the bonds that held it down. In a few seconds it had freed itself from its gigantic stem and floated upward with tremendous speed, its momentum carrying it into the stratosphere to a height of about sixty thousand feet.

But at that instant another mushroom, smaller in size than the first one, began emerging out of the pillar. It was as though the decapitated monster was growing a new head.

As the first mushroom floated off into the blue it changed its shape into a flowerlike form, its giant petals curving downward, creamy white outside, rose-colored inside. It still retained that shape when we last gazed at it from a distance of about two hundred miles.

The boiling pillar of many colors could also be seen at that distance, a giant mountain of jumbled rainbows, in travail. Much living substance had gone into those rainbows.

The quivering top of the pillar protruded to a great height through the white clouds, giving the appearance of a monstrous prehistoric creature with a ruff around its neck, a fleecy ruff extending in all directions, as far as the eye could see.

We landed in Okinawa in the afternoon, our tanks nearly empty, and there, to our great relief, was No. 77. On landing, two of its motors had stopped dead halfway down the runway for lack of fuel.

As No. 77 approached Okinawa, the pilot had signaled that he was coming in for an emergency landing without circling the field. To get immediate clearance he sent down the proper flare, which, however, failed to work. So his crew shot off all the flares in the B-29 vocabulary, including the one signifying "Wounded aboard." They were met by all the emergency paraphernalia and personnel on the field—ambulances, crash wagons, doctors, Red Cross workers, and priests.

While we were refueling we learned that the Soviet Union had entered the war against Japan.

The feeling of incredulity that two small bombs had devastated Hiroshima and Nagasaki persisted even in the highest military circles. Shortly after the Nagasaki mission, I was present when Lieutenant General Spaatz, then commander of the Pacific Strategic Air Forces, and several other high-ranking Air Force officers were being guided by young Dr. Charles P. Baker of Cornell University through the bomb assembly building. They were shown, among other things, the container in which the explosive material for the Nagasaki bomb had been delivered. Its small size puzzled General Spaatz.

"You mean," he said, "this container carried the fuse that set off a chain reaction in the atmosphere?"

"Oh no, General," said the very much surprised Dr. Baker. "This was it. The entire explosion came from the material in this container."

"Young man," said General Spaatz in the manner of a man too wise to be taken in, "you may believe it. I don't."

. . . .

Victims

John Hersey wrote an early account about the victims of the bombing of Hiroshima that remains a classic. It focuses almost entirely on six survivors, alternating between their stories. This selection has been organized to present a portion of Hersey's narrative about one of them.

Source: John Hersey, *Hiroshima* (New York: Alfred A. Knopf, 1946), pp. 18-21, 33-35, 61-62, and 74. Copyright © 1946 and renewed 1974 by John Hersey. Reprinted by permission of Alfred A. Knopf, Inc. Originally appeared in *The New Yorker*.

. . . .

On the train on the way into Hiroshima from the country, where he lived with his mother, Dr. Terufumi Sasaki, the Red Cross Hospital surgeon, thought over an unpleasant nightmare he had had the night before. His mother's home was in Mukaihara, thirty miles from the city, and it took him two hours by train and tram to reach the hospital. He had slept uneasily all night and had wakened an hour earlier than usual, and, feeling sluggish and slightly feverish, had debated whether to go to the hospital at all; his sense of duty finally forced him to go, and he had started out on an earlier train than he took most mornings. . . .

At the terminus, he caught a streetcar at once. (He later calculated that if he had taken his customary train that morning, and if he had had to wait a few minutes for the streetcar, as often happened, he would have been close to the center at the time of the explosion and would surely have perished.) He arrived at the hospital at seven-forty and reported to the chief surgeon. A few minutes later, he went to a room on the first floor and drew blood from the arm of a man in order to perform a Wassermann test. The laboratory containing the incubators for the test was on the third floor. With the blood specimen in his left hand, walking in a kind of distraction he had felt all morning, probably because of the dream and his restless night, he started along the main corridor on his way toward the stairs. He was one step beyond an open window when the light of the bomb was reflected, like a gigantic photographic flash, in the corridor. He ducked down on one knee and said to himself, as only a Japanese would, "Sasaki, *gambare!* Be brave!" Just then (the building was 1,650 yards from the center), the blast ripped through the hospital. The glasses he was wearing flew off his face; the bottle of blood crashed against one wall; his Japanese slippers zipped out from under his feet—but otherwise, thanks to where he stood, he was untouched.

Dr. Sasaki shouted the name of the chief surgeon and rushed around to the man's office and found him terribly cut by glass. The hospital was in horrible confusion: heavy partitions and ceilings had fallen on patients, beds had overturned, windows had blown in and cut people, blood was spattered on the walls and floors, instruments were everywhere, many of the patients were running about screaming, many more lay dead. (A colleague working in the laboratory to which Dr. Sasaki had been walking was dead; Dr. Sasaki's patient, whom he had just left and who a few moments before had been dreadfully afraid of syphilis, was also dead.) Dr. Sasaki found himself the only doctor in the hospital who was unhurt.

Dr. Sasaki, who believed that the enemy had hit only the building he was in, got bandages and began to bind the wounds of those inside the hospital; while outside, all over Hiroshima, maimed and dying citizens turned their unsteady steps toward the Red Cross Hospital to begin an invasion that was to make Dr. Sasaki forget his private nightmare for a long, long time.

. . . .

The lot of Drs. Fujii, Kanda, and Machii right after the explosion—and, as these three were typical, that of the majority of the physicians and surgeons of Hiroshima—with their offices and hospitals destroyed, their equipment scattered, their own bodies incapacitated in varying degrees, explained why so many citizens who were hurt went untended and why so many who might have lived died. Of a hundred and fifty doctors in the city, sixty-five were already dead and most of the rest were wounded. Of 1,780 nurses, 1,654 were dead or too badly hurt to work. In the biggest hospital, that of the Red Cross, only six doctors out of thirty were able to function, and only ten nurses out of more than two hundred. The sole uninjured doctor on the Red Cross Hospital staff was Dr. Sasaki. After the explosion, he hurried to a storeroom to fetch bandages. This room, like everything he had seen as he ran through the hospital, was chaotic—bottles of medicines thrown off shelves and broken, salves spattered on the walls, instruments strewn everywhere. He grabbed up some bandages and an unbroken bottle of mercurochrome, hurried back to the chief surgeon, and bandaged his cuts. Then he went out into the corridor and began patching up the wounded patients and the doctors and nurses there. He blundered so without his glasses that he took a pair off the face of a wounded nurse, and although they only approximately compensated for the errors of his vision, they were better than nothing. (He was to depend on them for more than a month.)

Dr. Sasaki worked without method, taking those who were nearest him first, and he noticed soon that the corridor seemed to be getting more and more crowded. Mixed in with the abrasions and lacerations which most people in the hospital had suffered, he began to find dreadful burns. He realized then that casualties were pouring in from outdoors. There were so many that he began to pass up the lightly wounded; he decided that all he could hope to do was to stop people from bleeding to death. Before long, patients lay and crouched on the floors of the wards and the laboratories and all the other rooms, and in the corridors, and on the stairs, and in the front hall, and under the portocochère, and on the stone front steps, and in the driveway and courtyard, and for blocks each way in the streets outside. Wounded people supported maimed people; disfigured families leaned together. Many people were vomiting. A tremendous number of schoolgirls—some of those who had been taken from their classrooms to work outdoors, clearing fire lanes—crept into the hospital. In a city of two hundred and forty-five thousand, nearly a hundred thousand people had been killed or doomed at one blow; a hundred thousand more were hurt. At least ten thousand of the wounded made their way to the best hospital in town, which was altogether unequal to such a trampling, since it had only six hundred beds, and they had all been occupied. The people in the suffocating crowd inside the hospital wept and cried, for Dr. Sasaki to hear, "*Sensei!* Doctor!," and the less seriously wounded came and pulled at his sleeve and begged him to go to the aid of the worse wounded. Tugged here and there in his stockinged feet, bewildered by the numbers, staggered by so much raw flesh, Dr. Sasaki lost all sense of profession and stopped working as a skillful surgeon and a sympathetic man; he became an automaton, mechanically wiping, daubing, winding, wiping, daubing, winding.

. . . .

By nightfall, ten thousand victims of the explosion had invaded the Red Cross Hospital, and Dr. Sasaki, worn out, was moving aimlessly and dully up and down the stinking corridors with wads of bandage and bottles of mercurochrome, still wearing the glasses he had taken from the wounded nurse, binding up the worst cuts as he came to them. Other doctors were putting compresses of saline solution on the worst burns. That was all they could do. After dark, they worked by the light of the city's fires and by candles the ten remaining nurses held for them. Dr. Sasaki had not looked outside the hospital all day; the scene inside was so terrible and so compelling that it had not occurred to him to ask any questions about what had happened beyond the windows and doors. Ceilings and partitions had fallen; plaster, dust, blood, and vomit were everywhere. Patients were dying by the hundreds, but there was nobody to carry away the corpses. Some of the hospital staff distributed biscuits and rice balls, but the charnel-house smell was so strong that few were hungry. By three o'clock the next morning, after nineteen straight hours of his gruesome work, Dr. Sasaki was incapable of dressing another wound. He and some other survivors of the hospital staff got straw mats and went outdoors —thousands of patients and hundreds of dead were in the yard and on the driveway—and hurried around behind the hospital and lay down in hiding to snatch some sleep. But within an hour wounded people had found them; a complaining circle formed around them: "Doctors! Help us! How can you sleep?" Dr. Sasaki got up again and went back to work. Early in the day, he thought for the first time of his mother, at their country home in Mukaihara, thirty miles from town. He usually went home every night. He was afraid she would think he was dead.

. . . .

At the Red Cross Hospital, Dr. Sasaki worked for three straight days with only one hour's sleep. On the second day, he began to sew up the worst cuts, and right through the following night and all the next day he stitched. Many of the wounds were festered. Fortunately, someone had found intact a supply of *narucopon*, a Japanese sedative, and he gave it to many who were in pain. Word went around among the staff that there must have been something peculiar about the great bomb, because on the second day the vice-chief of the hospital went down in the basement to the vault where the X-ray plates were stored and found the whole stock exposed as they lay. That day, a fresh doctor and ten nurses came in from the city of Yamaguchi with extra bandages and antiseptics, and the third day another physician and a dozen more nurses arrived from Matsue—yet there were still only eight doctors for ten thousand patients. In the afternoon of the third day, exhausted from his foul tailoring, Dr. Sasaki became obsessed with the idea that his mother thought he was dead. He got permission to go to Mukaihara. He walked out to the first suburbs, beyond which the electric train service was still functioning, and reached home late in the evening. His mother said she had known he was all right all along; a wounded nurse had stopped by to tell her. He went to bed and slept for seventeen hours.

. . . .

Arata Osada was a fifty-eight-year-old Japanese educator who was in Hiroshima when the atomic bomb fell. For four months, he was in critical condition and then recovered. He subsequently focused on peace education. In 1951, he compiled a collection of essays about the atomic bombing from many who had lived through it as children. Here is one to represent them all. Yohko Kuwabara had been a seventh grader in 1945 and was a twelfth grader when she wrote it.

Source: Yohko Kuwabara, untitled essay in *Children of Hiroshima*, [compiled by Arata Osada, edited by Yoichi Fukushima; original translation by Arata Osada subsequently edited by IEC Inc.] (Tokyo: Publishing Committee for "Children of Hiroshima," 1980; reprint, London: Taylor & Francis Ltd., 1981), pp. 260-63.

Work is steadily going on to rebuild the Hiroshima that was completely destroyed in an instant. Although six years have gone by, thoughts of that day still leave me with a feeling of fierce resentment for the atom bomb which I will never forget.

It was a clear but sultry morning. The midsummer sun was so bright it almost hurt my eyes. I looked at my watch. It was already past seven. 'I'll be late for school!' I started getting ready for school in a hurry. The awful scream of the air-raid siren began to echo across the morning sky, but the all-clear signal was given soon after. I left home and rushed over the dry and dusty asphalt to the Yamaguchi-cho streetcar stop. After I had waited thirty or forty minutes, a streetcar bound for Koi pulled up, already packed. Everyone at the stop moved toward the door at once, pushing and shoving. It looked as if I would not be able to get on, no matter how hard I tried. The streetcar suddenly started off, with someone perched with only one foot on the step. Someone shouted, "Stop! Stop! It's dangerous!" The streetcar came to an abrupt stop after about five yards, and again the people struggled madly to get on. Two or three more people got on, and it started off once more. I was one of the two or three. I pushed my way through until I was standing behind the driver. Through the windshield I looked at the pedestrians hurrying on their way, and soon we got to Hatchobori.

Just then, I was blinded for a moment by a piercing flash of bright light, and the air filled with yellow smoke like poison gas. Momentarily, it got so dark I couldn't see anything. There was a loud, dull, thunderous noise. The inside of my mouth was gritty, as if there were sand in it, and my throat hurt. As it started getting lighter, I desperately tried to pull the door

57

open, but couldn't. In the dim light, I saw an electricity pole, with severed wires dangling from it, lying in front of the streetcar. I turned around and was astonished. There was no one else in the streetcar! Everyone else had already gone out by the rear door. Electric wires lay coiled on the ground like barbed wire entanglements. Red flames were leaping from the windows of the Fukuya Department Store. I picked my way through the rubble and made it out to the main street. I saw a two-year-old child with blood all over him, crying in pain for his mother. I thought of my own mother and of going home. I looked to the east. An undescribable black thunder cloud was rolling upward. 'It's hopeless!' I thought as I stood there dumbfounded for a moment. Then I looked down at myself. Gone was the bag I had been carrying in my hand. Gone were the clogs I had been wearing. All I had left was the first-aid bag on my shoulder. I heard children crying, buildings collapsing, men and women screaming. I saw the bright red of blood and people with dazed expressions on their faces trying to get away. Where should I go? I ran after the other people. I crossed the West Parade Ground and finally found myself on the river bank behind Sentei.

Soon after, the houses on both sides of the river began to burn. I swam across the river to a strip of sand on the other side, and dropped to the ground, exhausted. The wind got stronger, and it started raining something like ink. This strange rain came down hard out of the gray sky, like a thundershower and the drops stung as if I were being hit by pebbles. All through this, sparks kept falling on me. I got up to go to the river, but a gust of wind blew me down. 'I've had it!' I lay down on my stomach with both hands over my face. Hot sparks fell on my bare feet but I could not change position to brush them off because I was afraid of being blown about by the wind. Big sparks like lumps of fire fell like rain. I couldn't take it any longer and stood up, determined to get to the water, but I was knocked down again by the strong, hot wind. How can I ever describe on paper what I went through then? Desperation and despair went through my mind one after the other.

I don't know how many hours passed after that. The hot wind had died away and it was getting dark. I wandered around by myself, looking for a place to sleep. I walked in the direction of Koi, along the street the streetcar had run on, through Hatchobori, and over Aioi Bridge. There were fires on both sides of the street.

I had a long stay in the hospital afterwards, with my parents nursing me. My life was miraculously saved, though I cannot say whether it was for better or worse.

People say that memories of the past are pleasant, but I, whose fate was completly changed by the atom bomb, will never forget the anger I feel for it, no matter how hard I try not to think of it.

What was the cause of this great tragedy? War, of course. No one wants a tragedy like this to occur again, ever, anywhere in the world. It is my hope that by telling the people of the world of the horror of the atom bomb, and the pain it caused, I will have helped in making a new, kind-hearted world, where everyone can live without fear. If such a world full of hope for everyone is to be made through the prayers and efforts of the people of the world, then it is the duty of the people of Hiroshima to have the strength and resolution to lead others in this endeavor. In closing, I want to call out, 'People of the world, do not let what Hiroshima has experienced ever be repeated!'

The World Transformed

Before World War II, J. Robert Oppenheimer was well known within the community of academic science, but essentially unknown beyond its boundaries. In the period following the war, he rose rapidly to become a highly visible statesman of science. As well as anyone else, Oppenheimer understood that he had been a central actor in taking the world somewhere it had never been before. One of his postwar speaking engagements was at the University of Pennsylvania's graduation exercises in February of 1946. This selection, a portion of the resulting publication, presents some of his observations and insights.

Source: J. Robert Oppenheimer, "The Atom Bomb and College Education," *The General Magazine and Historical Chronicle*, The General Alumni Society, University of Pennsylvania, Volume 48 (Summer 1946), pp. 262-65. Copyright © 1946 by The General Alumni Society, University of Pennsylvania. Reprinted by permission of The University of Pennsylvania Archives.

A great many wise and many more foolish things have of course been said on the subject of atomic weapons and atomic energy; but they have not managed quite to divest it of its importance, its urgency, or even entirely of its interest. . . .

. . . .

. . . The events that climaxed the end of this last terrible war—the release of atomic energy in a weapon of war—have shown, as not very often before, how essential is man's ability wisely to decide, man's ability to use for his welfare and his freedom, and not his destruction—the new powers, the new alternatives, of an advancing mastery of nature.

Do not mistake me: atomic bombs were never the purpose or the goal of science. The fundamental phenomena of nuclear fission and nuclear transmutations on which they were based, turned up, without solicitation, almost as a by-product of the great efforts of the last decades to extend and deepen our knowledge of the physical world. The technical, the technological, the industrial brilliance that went into the actual large scale development of atomic weapons, are precisely those that have done most, on the one hand to increase our understanding of nature, and on the other to enrich men's lives and increase man's freedom. It is appropriate, it is in my opinion a most urgent and binding obligation, to resolve, in all ways that lie within our power, so to choose our ways of life that atomic weapons may never be used again in anger, in the indiscriminate devastation of an atomic war. It is in my opinion contrary to all human wisdom to repudiate, to restrict, or to cause to perish the two great human developments—science and technology—of which atomic weapons are an almost incidental consequence. For these developments represent much of the hope of the world, in man's desire for knowledge, and such power as comes with that—for freedom from want and from fear, for a life rich in opportunity and the possibilities of conscious and thoughtful decision.

It has been said that many who worked on the great atomic energy projects, hoped that atomic weapons would be impossible. I have not shared that hope; it is based on man's distrust of man. There were, even after the fundamental discovery of fission, many crucial experiments that might have shown that a chain reaction could not work. At first, for instance, it was not clear that not enough neutrons would be available from one nuclear fission to propagate the fission reaction at an ever-increasing intensity. Even when that point was settled, there was a fundamental question of timing—for an explosive chain reaction could not occur if there were even a minute delay between the process of fission and the emission of the neutrons that propagate the chain. There was a little melancholy talk among the scientists when that question was answered by experiment, and there were no such delays; but this talk never seemed to me very honest, never seemed to me in accord with our real conviction. And when the academic doubts, the questions of principle were settled, and we set to work on the intricate enterprise of designing and making bombs, and were ready, in the desert stretch of the Jornad[a] del Muerto, to try one out, the issue was a greatly different one. We were quite sure then that atomic bombs could be made, that some day one would be made. The issue then was whether we had made this one right. If it had failed, we would have tried again, learning what we could from the failure. But we would have taken failure very hard, and not only because of its possible effects on the war. We were concerned, we were rightly and somewhat desperately concerned, that these weapons, which would we knew some day be a possibility, should be manifest to all men to see and understand, that they might know what future war would be, that they might bring to bear this knowledge, and the insight that derives from it, in shaping their ways. It would not have been a better world if the unrealized possibility of these terrible weapons had been a secret shadow on our future.

When it went off, in the New Mexico dawn, that first atomic bomb, we thought of Alfred Nobel, and his hope, his vain hope, that dynamite would put an end to wars. We thought of the legend of Prometheus, of that deep sense of guilt in man's new powers, that reflects his recognition of evil, and his long knowledge of it. We knew that it was a new world, but even more we knew that novelty was itself a very old thing in human life, that all our ways are rooted in it.

We knew then, too, as everyone has come since to know, that this was not a small thing. We knew it meant a vast increase in the destructiveness of war, not for us after our late experience an unimaginable increase, but in the true sense a revolutionary one. We knew it would never again cost as much to kill a million people, to ruin their homes and works and lives. We knew how dim and inadequate the prospects were of defense. We knew that this development, rooted in a universal science and in a technology well on its way to becoming world wide, could not for very long be ours alone. We knew that it was a changed world, and that by our participation in it, we had become committed, for all that it might take of us, to helping our fellow men to know the facts and bases of that change.

It did not take atomic weapons to make war terrible. The men who have been in combat, the men and women who have seen the material and the human wreckage of Europe and of Asia, can tell us that. It did not take atomic weapons to make man want peace, a peace that would last. But the atomic bomb was the turn of the screw. It has made the prospect of future war unendurable. It has led us up those last few steps to the mountain pass; and beyond there is a different country.

. . . .

Suggestions for Further Reading

The literature on the Manhattan Project and kindred topics is extensive. The space available here for presenting it is quite limited. The reader is certainly referred to the books and articles from which this anthology's selections have been culled, and, as a corollary, to the updated version of Hiroshima *with a final chapter, "The Aftermath," which John Hersey added four decades after his initial effort. The new version was originally published in 1985 by Alfred A. Knopf, Inc. In addition, here are several other books recommended as good next steps. Those by McGeorge Bundy and Richard Rhodes both have comprehensive bibliographies that contain material with dates of publication extending into the 1980s.*

Bundy, McGeorge. *Danger and Survival: Choices about the Bomb in the First Fifty Years.* New York: Random House, 1988.
> An excellent review and analysis of public policy on nuclear weapons. The author is a distinguished scholar who has also served as an advisor in the high councils of American government.

Deitch, Kenneth M., and Joseph R. Yeamans. *J. Robert Oppenheimer and the Birth of the Atomic Age.* Lowell, MA: Discovery Enterprises, Ltd., in preparation.
> A concise biography following Oppenheimer into and through his work on the Manhattan Project, his postwar achievements and subsequent tribulations, and the later phases of his remarkable life.

Rhodes, Richard. *The Making of the Atomic Bomb.* New York: Simon and Schuster, 1986.
> A brilliant, panoramic account. With great finesse, Rhodes has blended the relevant history, science, and biography. High among the book's innumerable assets is its absorbing portrait of Leo Szilard.

Smyth, Henry DeWolf. *Atomic Energy for Military Purposes: The Official Report on the Development of the Atomic Bomb under the Auspices of the United States Government.* Princeton: Princeton University Press, 1945.
> An extremely illuminating report, first issued by the government almost immediately after the project had become public knowledge. Princeton University Press subsequently made it available in large numbers.

Finally, an organization helpful to those seeking information about the Manhattan Project and related matters is: Los Alamos Historical Society, P.O. Box 43, Los Alamos, New Mexico 87544.